The Right to Rule

Written by Peter Rees
Illustrated by John Bennett

Scotland

My name is Annabel. I live in Glasgow, Scotland. The Scottish are very proud people. We have our own parliament, but we are part of the United Kingdom, and its government still has control over Scotland. I think we should be an independent country and make all our own rules.

2

the last

www.heinemannlibrary.co.uk
Visit our website to find out more
information about Heinemann
Library books.

To order:
☎ Phone +44 (0) 1865 888066
🖹 Fax +44 (0) 1865 314091
💻 Visit www.heinemannlibrary.co.uk

Heinemann Library is an imprint of **Capstone Global Library Limited**, a company incorporated in England and Wales having its registered office at 7 Pilgrim Street, London, EC4V 6LB – Registered company number: 6695582

"Heinemann Library" is a registered trademark of Pearson Education Limited, under licence to Capstone Global Library Limited

Text © Capstone Global Library Limited 2009
First published by Weldon Owen Education Inc. in 2008
First published in hardback in the United Kingdom in 2009
The moral rights of the proprietor have been asserted.

Written by Peter Rees
Edited by Briony Hill
Designed by Matthew Alexander
Original illustrations © Weldon Owen Education Inc. 2008
Illustrated by John Bennett
Picture research by Jamshed Mistry
Originated by Weldon Owen Education Inc.

Printed in China through Colorcraft Ltd., Hong Kong

Acknowledgements
We would like to thank the following for permission to reproduce photographs: Big Stock Photo: Kevin Tan (currency, p. 19); Getty Images (Glasgow, pp. 2–3; UK protestors, Montenegro football, p. 21); Jennifer and Brian Lupton (girl, p. 2; students, pp. 22–23; p. 24); Photodisc (background, pp. 22–23); Photolibrary (p. 1; Edinburgh Festival, pp. 18–19); Tranz: Corbis (pp. 14–15; New Scottish Parliament building, pp. 17–18; p. 20; gas plant, p. 21); Reuters (cover)

ISBN 978-0-431179-61-2 (hardback)
13 12 11 10 09
10 9 8 7 6 5 4 3 2 1

J320·941

1774730

British Library Cataloguing in Publication Data
Rees, Peter, 1966-
   The right to rule: devolution. – (Worldscapes)
320.8-dc22
A full catalogue record for this book is available from the British Library.

Every effort has been made to contact copyright holders of material reproduced in this book. Any omissions will be rectified in subsequent printings if notice is given to the publishers.

Disclaimer
All the Internet addresses (URLs) given in this book were valid at the time of going to press. However, due to the dynamic nature of the Internet, some addresses may have changed, or sites may have changed or ceased to exist since publication. While the author and Publishers regret any inconvenience this may cause readers, no responsibility for any such changes can be accepted by either the author or the Publishers.

Contents

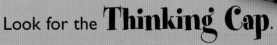

Look for the **Thinking Cap**.
When you see this picture, you will find
a problem to think about and write about.

Independence day

Grounded

Robbie wasn't too pleased about being grounded. After all, as he tried to explain to his parents, he was entirely innocent. He had merely been testing a brilliant new invention in the backyard. The invention consisted of an elastic cord attached to a golf ball so that golfers could practise their swing and the ball would return like a boomerang. It wasn't Robbie's fault that the cord had snapped – even that other great Scottish inventor, Alexander Graham Bell, probably had his off days. Nor was it his fault that Mr McBride across the street happened to be standing at his open window practising the bagpipes.

Robbie *certainly* couldn't have foreseen that the flying golf ball would smack into the bagpipes, causing them to emit a noise so ghastly that Mrs McKenzie next door dropped a freshly boiled **haggis** on Mr McKenzie's foot.

haggis Scottish dish consisting of the minced heart, lungs and liver of a sheep or calf and cooked in a sheep's stomach

Famous Scots include Alexander Graham Bell, the inventor of the telephone, and John Logie Baird, who made the first television.

Robbie was lying on his bed, listening to the radio and lamenting his bad luck, when a news item caught his attention. A group of protesters were demanding Scottish independence. The report said that the protesters wanted Scotland to leave the United Kingdom and become a sovereign nation. It gave Robbie an idea. 'That's it,' he thought, suddenly excited.

A declaration

A few minutes later, Robbie marched into the living room and declared that, from now on, his bedroom was an independent country. His father looked up from his newspaper. 'Oh, aye?' he said. 'What's the name of this so-called country?'

'Robbieland,' said Robbie, 'and it has its own laws. That means I no longer have to abide by *your* unfair rules, which means I'm no longer grounded.'

Robbie's mother came in from the garden. 'Did you hear, dear?' said his father. 'Our Robbie's gone independent.'

'Is that right, Robbie?' said his mother.

'That's right,' said Robbie. 'Now if you'll excuse me, I'm going out.' He headed for the front door.

'Och, not so fast,' said his father. 'We'll need to see your passport.'

Robbie stopped. 'Passport?'

'Aye, passport,' said his mother, as if it were perfectly normal for a boy to need a passport to walk through his own house. 'You *are* visiting from another country, are you not?'

Robbie hadn't expected this. Still, it shouldn't be a problem. He could easily whip up an official Robbieland passport on his computer. 'I'll show you my passport,' he said, feeling suddenly hungry. 'Right after lunch.'

His parents shook their heads. 'Not in *our* kitchen,' they said. 'Not without a passport.'

In addition to English, Scotland is home to two distinct languages: Scots and Scottish Gaelic. Neither is widely spoken today, but some words, such as the Gaelic words 'och' and 'aye' (both of which are forms of 'yes') are still used by the Scottish.

A cash concern

On his computer, Robbie put the finishing touches on his new passport and hit the 'print' button. His parents wouldn't get the better of him!

He signed the printed passport, crossed the border (his bedroom doorway) and handed the passport to his mother. Beneath a photo of Robbie, the passport read: '*His Highness, Robbie MacNab, Supreme Ruler of the free and independent nation of Robbieland, requests that the holder of this passport be allowed to pass without delay. Also, that he be **exempt** from dishwashing, lawnmowing and other boring and unfair chores.*'

His mother inspected the passport. 'Aye, it seems to be in order.'

'Thanks,' said Robbie. 'Now, if you will kindly give me my allowance, I'll be on my way.'

In the next room, Robbie's father snorted.

'Allowance?' his mother said with a smirk. 'Independent nations don't get allowances! They have to make their own way in the world.'

Robbie was stunned. This was a serious setback. It took a few moments for his cunning brain to devise a plan.

exempt freed from duty

Back in his room, Robbie set to work. He drew an especially flattering picture of himself and scanned it into his computer. He enlarged the drawing, and below it he typed '30p'. Then he printed off a poster that read, 'For Sale: Rare Postage Stamps. £3 per sheet of 10. Apply within'. He stuck the poster in his window so that it could be read from the street.

As he waited for the money to come rolling in, Robbie glanced around his bedroom. Clothes, books, engineering magazines and half-finished inventions lay everywhere. It wasn't right for an independent nation to be in such a horrible state.

Soon after, Robbie's father poked his head around the door and found Robbie cleaning his room without being asked, bribed or threatened. The shock left him quite speechless.

The prowler

That night, Robbie woke to feel a raspy tongue licking his face. 'Get off, Dougal!' he said, pushing away the family cat. Dougal meowed and jumped onto the window sill. Looking out the window, Robbie glimpsed a dark, hunched figure creeping across the front lawn. A prowler!

What should he do? The prowler might be dangerous. He might be an escaped convict on the run from the police. One thing was for sure – this was not a situation for a small, independent country to tackle on its own. Strong allies were required. Still in his pyjamas, Robbie dashed into the living room where his parents were watching TV.

'You're supposed to be in bed, young Robbie!' grumbled his father.

'Prowler!' Robbie whispered. 'Outside!'

His parents leaped to their feet. They all peered out the window. The prowler was still there, wandering in circles, scratching his head as if lost. As they watched, he disappeared around the corner of the house. 'Better call the police, dear,' said Robbie's father. His mother picked up the phone, but before she could call, there was a knock at the back door.

'Stay here,' said Robbie's father, going to the rear of the house. Robbie and his mother heard him open the back door, leaving the safety chain attached. There was the sound of voices. Then his father came back.

'You've got a visitor,' he said to Robbie.

'Me?' said Robbie. Who on Earth would be visiting him at this time of night? A little shocked, he walked slowly to the back door. There stood a small, elderly man with a mop of white hair and thick, round glasses.

'Och, you must be Robbie,' the man said in a lively voice that made Robbie like him at once. 'I'm Professor Michael Carmichael, a stamp collector. Terribly sorry to wake you. I was out for a late stroll and I noticed your sign. I'd very much like to see your postage stamps.'

For a second, Robbie was speechless. He had no idea his advertising skills were so brilliant. Perhaps he would have a sales career.

'Go on, Robbie, go and get your stamps for the professor to look at,' said his mother. As Robbie turned to run upstairs to get the stamps from his kingdom, he could hear his parents chatting with the professor.

The treaty

The next morning, Robbie was feeling extremely smug and satisfied.

His parents were sitting near him in the kitchen. On the table lay a piece of paper. Robbie proudly announced that it was an International Treaty of Cooperation. On it was printed:

'We, the undersigned, hereby agree to the following:

1. Mr and Mrs MacNab shall provide the population of Robbieland with services including dinners, packed lunches, car rides to soccer on Saturday mornings and a weekly allowance.

2. In return, the population of Robbieland shall obey house rules, finish homework, make the bed and do everything else Mr and Mrs MacNab ask, without complaining.'

'Sign here, your Highness,' laughed Robbie's mother, handing him a pen after she and her husband signed.

'Son,' said his mother, suddenly sounding serious. 'I know you got this idea for independence from the protests in the news. It's great you're thinking about the issue. However, do you understand what independence means to the people of a country?'

Robbie was quiet. He thought about what freedom meant to him. He tried to imagine what it would mean to the Scots who were protesting. He wondered what other Scots might feel about independence, and if they agreed. 'I'll find out more about it,' he declared.

'Good idea, Robbie. Until then, long live Robbieland!'

Robbie beamed.

Put on your thinking cap

Write down your thoughts about the following questions. Then discuss them with a classmate.

1. Why did Robbie declare himself independent from his parents? Have you ever felt like Robbie did?

2. What problems did Robbie fail to foresee?

3. What lesson does Robbie learn about his relationship with his parents?

4. In what ways do you think children can be independent from parents? How much independence is too much, and how much is not enough?

5. As Robbie grows up he will naturally become more independent. How is Robbie's situation different from that of a dependent nation? How is it similar?

What's the issue?

In 2007, Scotland marked a special anniversary. It had been 300 years since Scotland had joined with its southern neighbour, England, to form Great Britain.

On 1 May 1707, the Scottish and English Parliaments were **dissolved** and a new Parliament of Great Britain was set up in London, England. The border between Scotland and England was opened to free trade.

Not everyone in Scotland celebrated the anniversary. To many, it commemorated the end of Scotland's proud history as a free and independent nation. Although a new Scottish Parliament was set up in 1999, it has only limited powers. Many important decisions are still made in London, hundreds of kilometres to the south.

For years, some Scottish have been saying that Scotland should leave Great Britain and become independent once more. Opinion polls have shown that many people on both sides of the Scottish–English border agree with them.

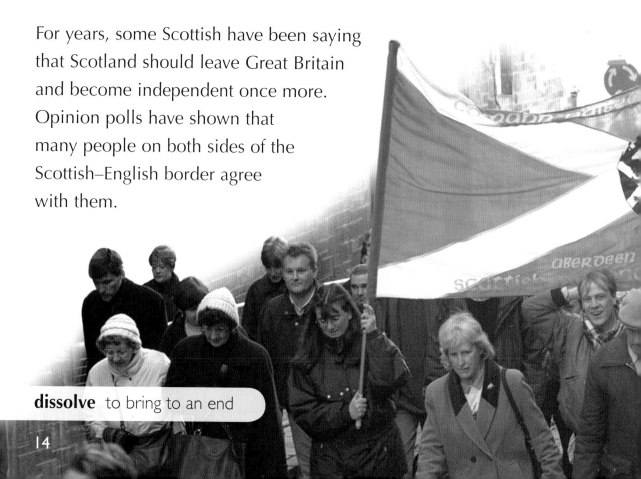

dissolve to bring to an end

Independent people

Over the centuries, Scotland earned a reputation for fierce independence, fighting many wars against its powerful neighbour, England.

At the start of the eighteenth century, England feared that Scotland might unite with France and invade England. To control Scotland, England banned the import of Scottish goods. This caused financial problems for Scotland, which was already short of money. England then offered Scotland money and free trade with England if it agreed to unite with England.

In 1603, King James VI of Scotland was made King James I of England. From that time on, British kings and queens have ruled over both countries.

Back then, most ordinary Scots strongly opposed the union. However, only the politicians in the Scottish Parliament were able to vote. In 1707, they voted for the union 110 votes to 69.

Some Scottish continue to protest for independence.

Great Britain is the island of England, Wales and Scotland. The United Kingdom is Great Britain plus Northern Ireland. Tony Blair and Gordon Brown, two recent prime ministers of the United Kingdom, were born in Scotland.

Devolution

In 1999, a new Scottish Parliament opened in Edinburgh, the capital of Scotland. The Parliament has wide powers over areas such as health, education, transport, the environment and law and justice. However, many important responsibilities are still reserved for the United Kingdom Parliament in London. For example, only the UK Parliament can create or abolish taxes. Foreign affairs, national security and defence decisions are also reserved for the UK Parliament.

This partial transfer of power is called devolution. Many people in Scotland believe devolution is not enough. They want nothing less than full independence for Scotland.

The new Scottish Parliament building opened in 2004.

The party that holds the most seats in the Scottish Parliament supports the move to independence. It has promised that a **referendum** will be held before 2010. The referendum will give the people of Scotland the opportunity to vote on the issue of independence.

More than 200 years ago, the United States won independence from Britain. Before the Revolutionary War, the 13 colonies in America were controlled by the British Parliament.

referendum issue submitted to the public to be decided upon by voting

Who pays?

Countries need to pay for the things they are expected to provide. In Scotland, the government provides free health care and education for all. Some people doubt that an independent Scotland could afford to pay for all these services. Scotland's economy is healthy. Unemployment is fairly low. Although some traditional industries have declined, newer ones, such as electronics, finance and tourism, are doing well. But population density is low, and many remote areas are less developed than the cities.

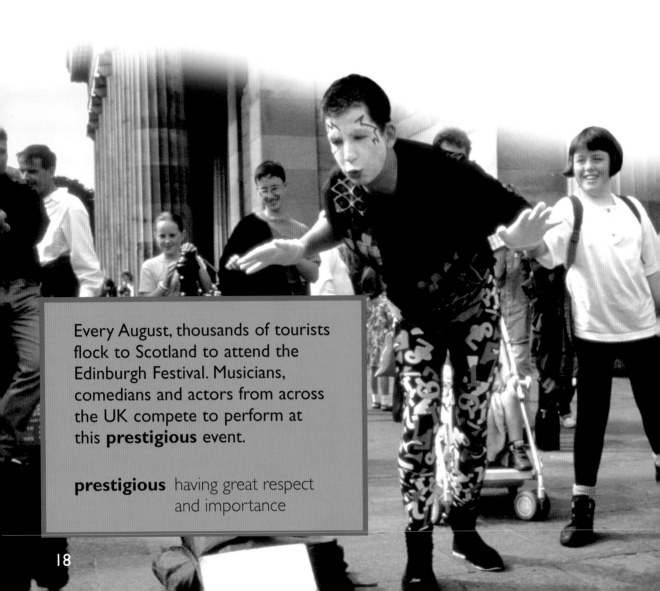

Every August, thousands of tourists flock to Scotland to attend the Edinburgh Festival. Musicians, comedians and actors from across the UK compete to perform at this **prestigious** event.

prestigious having great respect and importance

Many pro-independence Scots pin their hopes on oil. Off the coast of Scotland, there are huge oil reserves that could earn the country billions of pounds each year. But oil production has fallen in recent times, and the price of oil is often unstable. In the end, Scotland's best hope of future success may be its long tradition of producing inventive, hard-working people, such as the founding father of modern physics, Lord Kelvin.

From one union to another?

The United Kingdom has been a member of the European Union, or EU, since 1973. The EU is a powerful organisation of European countries. Countries in the EU trade freely and share open borders. They have many common laws, and some even have a shared currency, the Euro, or €. Less developed areas of Europe receive financial assistance from the EU.

If Scotland left the United Kingdom, it would probably apply to join the EU. However, it is not certain that an independent Scotland would immediately be able to join. It can take many years for countries to be accepted into this exclusive organisation.

Independence around the world

Setback for Quebec independence

CANADA – Voters in the Canadian province of Quebec have dealt a blow to Quebec's independence movement. The main pro-independence party only managed to come in third in a recent election. Quebec was founded by French settlers and is still mostly French speaking. Many French-speaking people in Quebec want partial independence from Canada, but most English-speaking Canadians oppose it.

Nobel prizewinner elected president

EAST TIMOR – José Ramos-Horta has won East Timor's first presidential election since the country became independent in 2002. Mr Ramos-Horta received the 1996 Nobel Peace Prize for his work in the independence movement. Since independence, the island nation has suffered from violence and poverty. Even so, more than 80 per cent of the population turned out to vote in the 2007 election.

Protesters call for the return of an English parliament

UNITED KINGDOM – A group of protesters marked the 300th anniversary of the formation of Great Britain with a petition calling for an English-only Parliament. The protesters point out that Wales, Scotland and Northern Ireland all have parliaments, leaving England the only country in the UK without a separate parliament.

Football team wins first ever match

MONTENEGRO – Montenegro's new football team celebrated its first ever game with a win over Hungary. Until 2006, Montenegro was part of the Serbia and Montenegro Union. Montenegro became independent less than two weeks after a referendum in which a majority of people voted in favour of the move.

Gas cut

BELARUS – A dispute between Russia and Belarus over the price of gas has caused tension. Although independent from Russia since 1991, Belarus's economy and culture are still closely tied to Russia. Large parts of Russian oil and gas exports to Europe pass through Belarus. Russia threatened to cut the supply, and now Belarus has to pay twice as much for gas.

What's your opinion?

Many of us like to be as independent as possible. We want to choose our friends, our jobs and where we go for lunch. But in other ways, we are dependent on others. We need doctors to help us when we are ill. We need an economy that provides jobs, and we need workers such as architects, engineers and builders to construct our homes and roads. No one can be completely independent from the people around them. Yet making our own decisions is important to us.

Just like individuals, countries prefer to make their own decisions. But again, they are also dependent on their neighbours being friendly, on importing what they need, and exporting what they want to sell.

International organisations, such as the European Union, try to find solutions to problems to benefit everyone. To become part of the EU, member states give up a small part of their independence and agree to follow EU rules in some matters of economy, trade, security and the environment.

- Do you think international organisations such as the EU are a good idea? Why or why not?

- In which situations do you think it's all right for a country to be told what to do?

- Which decisions should a country reach independently? Explain your answer.

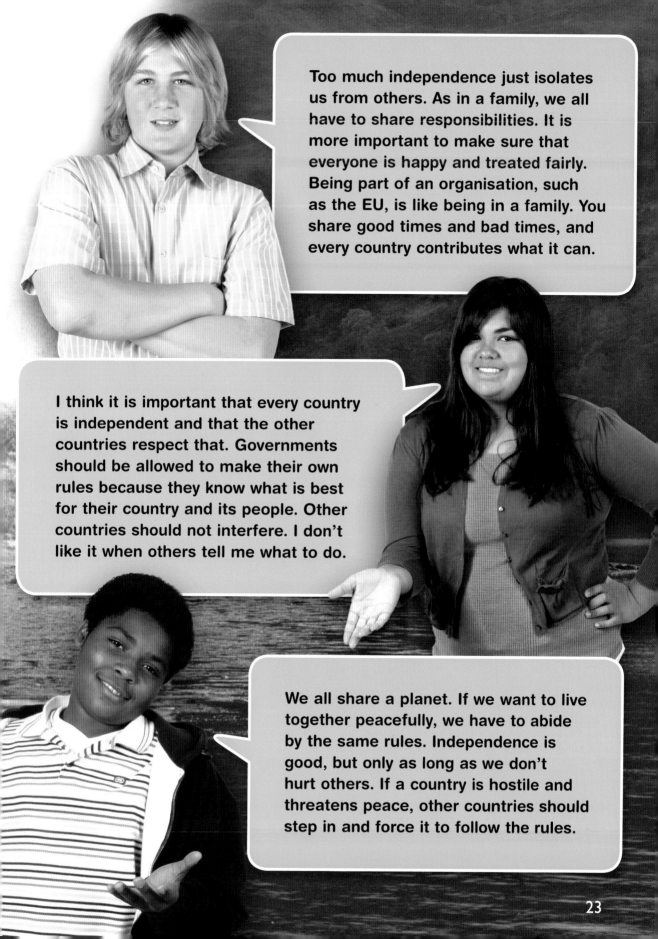

Too much independence just isolates us from others. As in a family, we all have to share responsibilities. It is more important to make sure that everyone is happy and treated fairly. Being part of an organisation, such as the EU, is like being in a family. You share good times and bad times, and every country contributes what it can.

I think it is important that every country is independent and that the other countries respect that. Governments should be allowed to make their own rules because they know what is best for their country and its people. Other countries should not interfere. I don't like it when others tell me what to do.

We all share a planet. If we want to live together peacefully, we have to abide by the same rules. Independence is good, but only as long as we don't hurt others. If a country is hostile and threatens peace, other countries should step in and force it to follow the rules.

Think tank

Do your own research at the library, on the Internet, or with a parent or teacher to find out more about independence issues and what people around the world are doing to gain and keep independence.

1 Find out about a country that has recently become independent. What challenges is the country facing so far? How is it doing better than before, and in what ways is it struggling?

2 Annexation means joining a country or territory to another state. Think of an independent country. What would be some benefits and problems for that country if it were annexed?

3 Imagine your town became independent from the rest of the country. What effects might this have on the people in your town, the businesses and the economy?

Glossary

dissolve to bring to an end

exempt freed from duty

haggis Scottish dish consisting of the minced heart, lungs and liver of a sheep or calf cooked in a sheep's stomach

prestigious having great respect and importance

referendum issue submitted to the public to be decided upon by voting

Index